The Terminator

Sean French

BRITISH FILM INSTITUTE

bfi

BFI PUBLISHING

First published in 1996 by the
British Film Institute
21 Stephen Street, London W1P 2LN

Copyright © Sean French 1996
Reprinted 1998
The British Film Institute exists to promote
appreciation, enjoyment, protection and
development of moving image culture in and
throughout the whole of the United Kingdom.
Its activities include the National Film and
Television Archive; the National Film Theatre;
the Museum of the Moving Image;
the London Film Festival; the production and
distribution of film and video; funding and
support for regional activities; Library and
Information Services; Stills, Posters and
Designs; Research; Publishing and Education;
and the monthly *Sight and Sound* magazine.

Designed by Andrew Barron &
Collis Clements Associates

Typeset in Garamond Simoncini
by Fakenham Photosetting Ltd

Printed in Great Britain by
Norwich Colour Print

British Library Cataloguing-in-Publication Data
A catalogue record for this book is available
from the British Library
ISBN 0-85170-553-7

Contents

Introduction

Other people, so I have read, treasure memorable moments in their lives: the time one climbed the Parthenon at sunrise, the summer night one met a lonely girl in Central Park and achieved with her a sweet and natural relationship, as they say in books. I too once met a girl in Central Park, but it is not much to remember. What I remember is the time John Wayne killed three men with a carbine as he was falling to the dusty street in *Stagecoach*, and the time the kitten found Orson Welles in the doorway in *The Third Man*.

Walker Percy, *The Movie-goer*, 1961

It could be said of Cameron that no one did so much to redeem the eighties genre of high-tech threat through the overlay of genuine human interest stories. But that description smacks of the formulaic. Perhaps it would be more to the point to ask who smothered so many promising stories with effects and apparatus?

David Thomson, *A Biographical Dictionary of Film*, 1994

With alphabetical serendipity, the entry after James Cameron in David Thomson's *Biographical Dictionary* is Cameron's polar opposite, artistically as well as literally, Jane Campion. Thomson rhapsodises over *The Piano*: 'The sense of place, of spirit, and of silence is Wordsworthian … rare poetry. … No one has better caught the mix of sensitivity and ferocity in the human imagination.' This is the sort of praise Campion's film asks for. With its systematic symbolism, its schematic characterisation, *The Piano* was manifestly conceived as a masterpiece and this intention is evident in every frame, in every carefully composed set-up. It is a film for adults.

How different from *The Terminator*, the sort of project that seems to have been developed without even the intention of being any good. The film's producers at Orion could scarcely have anticipated much from its writer-director. James Cameron had worked in various technical capacities for Roger Corman and had confirmed his lack of promise at the helm of a disastrous cheapo sequel to Joe Dante's *Piranha* (1978). His *Terminator* storyline was largely culled from time-travel ideas that had already been explored in TV science fiction shows like *The Outer Limits* and *Star Trek*. The film's star was an Austrian muscleman, a European import in the tradition of Anna Sten, who had already become a laughing-stock because of his inability to act and his ineradicable accent. ('To crush your enemies,' went one of his lines of dialogue in his previous film, as transcribed by Nigel Andrews in *True Myths: The Life and Times of Arnold Schwarzenegger,* 'To see dem driven before you and to hear de lamentation of de vimmin.') The action was heavily dependent on visual effects, yet the film was initially budgeted at a minuscule $4 million (less than the special effects budget alone for the same year's *Ghostbusters*), and raised to $6.5 million only with the greatest reluctance.

Even when the film had opened and been initially acclaimed, Cameron himself was ruefully modest in his expectations, telling *Film Comment* (January–February 1985), 'We know we're going to get stomped by the Christmas movies. *Dune, 2010,* … I'll be lining up to see them – why shouldn't everybody else?' *Dune*? *2010*? *Dune* is now remembered as David Lynch's $50 million disaster. Peter Hyams's *2010* isn't remembered by anybody except Cameron himself who has twice adapted its central conceit, according to which the computer HAL, the villain of the first film, comes good in the sequel. (Ian Holm's android betrays the crew in *Alien*, while Lance Henriksen's android sacrifices himself for Ripley in *Aliens*; and in *Terminator 2*, Schwarzenegger's cyborg is reprogrammed to protect John Connor instead of destroying him.)

Isn't there something wrong with symbolism as obtrusive as what Jane Campion presents us with in *The Piano*? If you want a real 'sense of silence' look instead at the first five minutes of Hawks's *Rio Bravo* (1959). Dean Martin's alcoholic Dude shows the depth of his degradation by scrabbling for a coin in the spittoon. John Wayne tries to save Martin from himself and is struck down by him. Claude Aikens commits murder and walks down the street to another bar. We hear the sound of the door swinging open offscreen. It is Wayne once more, with blood trickling down his face. Speaking the first words in the film, he arrests Aikens and sets in motion the drama. It is a magnificently bold piece of cinematic narrative, yet it doesn't call attention to itself in the way that more celebrated opening *tours de force* do, such as that of Welles's *Touch of Evil* or the parodic long opening take of Robert Altman's *The Player*.

Critics are preoccupied with themes of films, what they are 'about'. And if an obviously commercial, popular film should be found worthy of attention, then that must be because it has some serious themes as well. Is this so? *Rio Bravo* is about loyalty, honour and redemption, I suppose, but isn't it also about Angie Dickinson throwing the vase through the window as Ricky Nelson tosses the rifle to John Wayne and shoots two men while it's in the air? And Wayne rolling his cigarettes with one hand and constantly searching for a match? Dean Martin noticing blood dripping into his drink and turning and killing the murderer of Ward Bond in a single shot? It's about the aplomb with which Hawks and his cast can take the most clichéd of Western archetypes, a dancing girl, a comic Mexican, a drunk, a crippled old-timer, and make them strange and complex once more.

Maybe there are some films that work like a Henry James novel, as an organic whole, but most of the ones that matter to us are about moments, quirky details we take away from them and treasure, an odd cameo here, a funny line there, an audacious camera movement, an amusing cut, a dazzling special effect or a satisfyingly baroque machine-gun. 'You know your weapons, buddy,' as Dick Miller says to Schwarzenegger in the gun shop scene. Film is a visceral, kinetic form for which critical criteria largely derived from literature and the theatre are ill suited.

By his own account, James Cameron grew up writing stories and painting pictures. His interest in storytelling led him to a fusion of the two in comic books. Then he discovered the cinema and realised it was what he had been looking for: 'That's what a movie is. It's a visual medium with a narrative intent.' To put it another way, James Cameron was perfectly qualified to make a low-budget film called *The Terminator* into the most important and influential film of the 80s. As he told an interviewer from *Films and Filming* (August 1986) who questioned him about the cyborg's destruction of the police station: 'I suppose it's anti-authoritarian. Why not? It's also visual, it's dynamic, it's the ultimate extrapolation of conflict, it's what makes things exciting.'

Is this enough to make a film a classic? Does the word even make sense in regard to a film barely more than ten years old? In the preface to his edition of Shakespeare's plays, Dr Johnson knew what was required to earn status of that kind:

The Poet, of whose works I have undertaken the revision, may now begin to assume the dignity of an ancient, and claim the privilege of established fame and prescriptive veneration. He has long outlived his century, the term commonly fixed as the test of literary merit. Whatever advantages he might once derive from personal allusions, local customs, or temporary opinions, have for many years been lost; and every topic of merriment or motive of sorrow, which the modes of artificial life afforded him, now only obscure the scenes which they once illuminated. The effects of favour and competition are at an end; the tradition of his friendships and his enmities has perished; his works support no opinion with arguments, nor supply any faction with invectives; they can neither indulge vanity nor gratify malignity, but are read without any other reason than the desire of pleasure, and are therefore praised only as pleasure is obtained; yet, thus unassisted by interest or passion, they have passed through variations of taste and changes of manners, and, as they devolved from one generation to another, have received new honours at every transmission.

Perhaps *The Terminator* has earned similar status by outliving its decade, if not its century. This 1984 film was considered worthy of a sequel after a gap of no less than seven years. As I write, in early 1996, twelve years after its opening, you can still buy it on video. What greater demonstration of longevity could be required?

The methods by which critics find commercial, unpretentious films worthy of serious attention, and accord them classic status, would in themselves constitute something of a history of film criticism. The stages of appreciation might go something like the following: X is trash but it has a vitality which is lacking in more artistic films; X may seem to be trash to the snobbish but it actually has serious themes and issues just like an art film; X is trash, so what's wrong with trash, anyway? Why should we be grown up all the time? X is commercial, it's profitable, it's enjoyable, what more do you want from a film?

Pauline Kael's brilliant, and hugely influential, 1968 essay, 'Trash, Art and the Movies' (reprinted in *Going Steady: Film Writings, 1968–1969*) explored these ideas while deliberately taunting the moviegoers who like films to be serious works of art like *Blow-Up* or *2001*. She was also trying to return to the experience of the way we look at movies: 'There is so much talk now about the art of the film that we may be in danger of forgetting that most of the movies we enjoy are not works of art.' Cinema, 'the most total and encompassing art form we have', was a landscape we could walk into: 'The romance of movies is not just in those stories and those people on the screen but in the adolescent dream of meeting others who feel as you do about what you've seen. You do meet them, of course, and you know each other at once because you talk less about good movies than about what you love in bad movies.'

And somehow, like a landscape, the movies were just there, a resource that intelligent, independent-minded people could mine in search of the occasional nugget that would show that Hollywood was not entirely corrupt. Kael's distrust of flashy technique was so deep rooted that it sometimes seemed like a distrust of *any* technique, as if the best film-makers and performers were Rousseauesque, instinctual creatures who produced moments of genius like hummingbirds inadvertently catching a sunbeam for a moment. It was still the debate between pulp and art; it was just that Kael tipped the balance slightly towards pulp.

If *The Terminator* deserves to be called a classic, then this is because the film transcends that largely sterile debate. The mark of a serious SF movie used to be that at some point a scientist would give a speech about the future of humanity (Linda Hamilton delivers a parody of such a speech in *Terminator 2*). James Cameron makes no bid for that sort of significance, but he remains a semiotician of immense resource. If one suspects that Luis Buñuel might have smiled at the film, it is not because of any ideas the film articulates, and not just because of the reference to his *Un chien andalou* in the cyborg's operation on his own

eye, but that he might have been tickled by the idea of a machine that rots. If Andy Warhol might have approved of the film, it is not because of any experiments with form but because of its casting coup, humanising his friend Arnold Schwarzenegger and making him the biggest star in the world by turning him into an inexpressive robot.

And Fritz Lang might have grimly approved of a film that seems to preach peace while depicting a future of Hobbesian struggle for survival between psychopathic machines and a tribe of Nietzschean human warriors.

The Terminator remains as irreducible and unpalatable as it is viscerally enjoyable. Only one man has been able to tame and civilise it, and that, in his self-consciously respectable sequel, is James Cameron himself.

Above *Un chien andalou*

1 Beginnings

James Cameron and his co-screenwriter and producer, Gale Anne Hurd, first met in their mid-twenties, when they were both employed by Roger Corman. They were among the last graduates of the New World Pictures company before Corman sold it and moved on. To Cameron and Hurd, as to other aspiring film-makers from Francis Coppola in the 60s to Joe Dante in the 80s, Corman offered an opportunity: in return for a willingness to accept strict financial and creative constraints, they would have the chance to work on movies in a variety of capacities. It was the closest Hollywood had to a functioning apprenticeship system for directors and producers.

Hurd worked as a production assistant on two rousing thrillers directed by Lewis Teague and written by John Sayles: *The Lady in Red* (1979), a noirish tale about the ex-girlfriend of John Dillinger, and *Alligator* (1980), about a giant alligator terrorising an American town. Then she co-produced with Roger Corman *Smokey Bites the Dust* (1981), a trashy thick-eared work, for which the car-chase sequences were simply snipped out of earlier Corman films such as *Eat My Dust* (1976) and *Grand Theft Auto* (1977; this film was Ron Howard's directorial debut).

Cameron, in *Film Comment*, recalled his younger self as 'interested in photography and design-related special effects' and he reached his zenith at New World Pictures with five credits on *Battle Beyond the Stars*, a characteristic Corman project, transposing *The Magnificent Seven* into space. He did 'everything from special effects to production design to a little bit of second unit to post-production work as a matte artist'.

The influence of the Corman industrial process on Cameron and Hurd was decisive. The subject matter was restricted to familiar genres and past films were raw material to be imaginatively plundered. Movies had to be made quickly and cheaply, yet they discovered what could be achieved with the most limited of resources. There were few professional barriers. Everybody got involved with everything, and for Cameron this was crucial: 'You see with some filmmakers where they begin to delegate too much authority. They're not in control of the nuances that give texture to a film like *Das Boot*, let's say, where every scene and every shot has some thought behind it. People get the smell of a movie that is too glossy or too packaged. They tend to like underdog movies.'

In her famous jeremiad, 'Why Are Movies So Bad? or, The Numbers', first published in the *New Yorker* in June 1980, Pauline Kael lamented the results of using so many untrained and unprotected first-time directors, technically ignorant, unused to working with actors, ill-at-ease on a movie set. This was never to be Cameron's problem. By the time he went out on his own, he had a basic technical grasp of every aspect of modern film-making from operating the camera to the most arcane details of special effects. He could write a script and he could storyboard a scene. When he came to make his own films, he had a

Escape from New York

knowledge of everybody's job that gave him a more than nominal authority. He could maintain control from a distance with the knowledge that the material he had storyboarded, even if it was created by different people in different places, would ultimately cohere.

In 1981 Cameron supervised the special effects on John Carpenter's *Escape from New York*. This is set in a future in which New York City has become so squalid that it has been abandoned, sealed off

and turned into a prison. When the US president's plane crashes into
the city, Kurt Russell is sent in to extricate him. The initial idea was
compelling and the grungy setting was effective, but the story remained
curiously undeveloped.

In the same year, Cameron directed his first film, *Piranha II: The
Flying Killers*, a sequel in name only to the witty 1978 original by the
recent Corman graduate Joe Dante. It has far less in common with
Cameron's later work than any of the films he had previously worked on,
even before it was heavily recut by the Italian producer, partly to include
a sequence of half-naked women sunbathing on a yacht. Cameron
himself has only commented that he would have done anything that gave
him a chance to direct. It was an uninteresting and insignificant film
which did nothing for Cameron except give him the title of director.

Piranha II: The Flying Killers

2 Borrowings

According to James Cameron, *The Terminator* began as an image in his mind of a robot walking out of a fire. Probably he was remembering the scene in Fritz Lang's *Metropolis*, in which the robot imitation of Maria is burned at the stake and the metal machine beneath is revealed. It is not sufficient merely to say that *The Terminator* teems with echoes of this kind. It is built out of them.   *IN TERTEXTUALITY*

Cameron has been open about the cinematic memories that feed into his work. Soon after the release of *The Terminator*, he told an interviewer from *Cinefantastique* (October 1985): 'If I really think about the influences that helped shape the story, the entire feeling can be traced back to some '50s science fiction films and *Outer Limits* episodes. The thing that *The Outer Limits* had, that always impressed me visually, was its use of the deep focus *film noir* look of the '40s films and the German Expressionist movies of the '30s.' Parallels were speedily alleged with a specific 1964 episode of *The Outer Limits* called 'Soldier', written by Harlan Ellison, which Cameron was known to have seen. Further comparisons were made, during this interview, with a machine-against-man story also written by Ellison, 'I Have No Mouth and I Must Scream', which begins in words similar to the text at the beginning of *The Terminator*:

The Cold War started and became World War Three and just kept going. It became a big war, a very complex war, so they needed computers to handle it. They sank the first shafts and began building AM (Allied Mastercomputer) … and everything was fine until they had honeycombed the entire planet, adding this element and that element. … In rage, in frenzy, the machine had killed the human race. … With the innate loathing that all machines had always held for the weak, soft creatures who had built them, he had sought revenge.

Other resemblances were also asserted. Another 1964 *Outer Limits* episode, 'Demon with a Glass Hand', featured a time-travelling robot entrusted with the fate of the human race. In a famous *Star Trek* episode, 'City on the Edge of Forever', McCoy travels back to twentieth-century Earth and his arrival is reminiscent of Reese's in *The Terminator*, in a similar back alley witnessed by a down-and-out in a doorway. But isn't this an example of a resemblance caused by practical responses to the same problem? The time traveller has to arrive in a city, but if he appears in a busy street, there will be distracting complications that have nothing to do with the story. The same could be said of other resemblances. Cameron certainly knew Ellison's work, but his vision of a future conflict between man and the technology he has created goes back to Prometheus. More recently, the battle between machines and people had been dramatised in Kubrick's *Dr Strangelove* (1963) and

Metropolis

2001 (1968), in John Carpenter's *Dark Star* (1974) and in numerous episodes of *Star Trek*. The issue was concluded as murkily as it had begun. After tortuous, acrimonious legal proceedings, a settlement was reached with Ellison, the enactment of which has itself been a matter of constant dispute.

In the aftermath of a sudden success, accusations of this kind are routine. Not all of them are unjustified. Dorothy Parker famously said that the only 'ism' Hollywood understood was plagiarism. Studio lawyers prefer to use terms like *hommage* (using the word in French makes it seem more artistic), coincidence or even 'fragmented literal similarity'. In fact, the more examples are produced against *The Terminator*, the less damaging they seem. They merely demonstrate the degree to which these ideas formed a bottomless pool of material, available to anybody who could find a use for them.

In an ingenious essay identifying the archetypes used in *Casablanca*, Umberto Eco pointed out in his book *Faith in Fakes* that what *Casablanca* had done unconsciously, more recent films have done 'with extreme intertextual awareness'. He continued:

It would be semiotically uninteresting to look for quotations of archetypes in *Raiders* or in *Indiana Jones*: they were conceived within a metasemiotic culture, and what the semiotician can find in them is exactly what the directors put there. Spielberg and Lucas are semiotically nourished authors working for a culture of instinctive semioticians.

Like Spielberg and Lucas, Cameron belongs to a generation of cinematically literate directors who are highly conscious of what they are doing. Cameron can draw on anything, from *Un chien andalou*, when Schwarzenegger slices through his damaged eye, to the slasher movies that were so commercially successful in the early 80s. Accusations of plagiarism are beside the point. Like many artists in all fields, Cameron has considerable skill in finding things that have worked for other people or, more interestingly, that *haven't* worked for other people but can work for him.

A typical example is his obvious debt to Michael Crichton's debut film, *Westworld* (1973). This is about a Western theme park where adults can go and play at cowboys, shooting a robot who looks like Yul Brynner and bedding the local whores. When – as in Crichton's later *Jurassic Park*

– the exhibits turn on the guests, the hero is pursued by the vengeful
Brynner android. Cameron drew on two separate aspects of the film.
Crichton's most striking visual coup was to show us the world through
the android's electronic eyes, an electronic mosaic, a surprisingly
touching effect which enabled the audience to identify briefly with the
creature. Cameron borrowed the idea and enriched it in *The Terminator*,
and made even subtler use of it in the sequel. If the lesson of *The
Terminator* and *Westworld* was that to share a character's point of view is
necessarily to identify with it and even feel something for it, then one of
the logical methods of preventing any audience involvement with the
even more advanced cyborg that pursues Schwarzenegger is to deny us
any participation in his point of view. By contrast, Cameron makes more
detailed use of the old terminator's point of view and the film's most
poignant moment is a technological effect: after the terminator has sunk
himself into the vat of molten metal at the climax of *Terminator 2*, we
see his visual display crackle, collapse and fade to a dot.

Cameron's second use of the film arose from his recognition of
how an initially potent idea had remained oddly unsatisfying. In
Westworld, Crichton showed little interest in the details of how the
androids might plausibly work. It was this abnegation that stimulated
Cameron's imagination, as he told *Film Comment*: 'I was thinking of an
indestructible machine, an endo-skeleton design, which had never been
filmed as such. We'd had things like *Westworld*, where Yul Brynner's face
falls off and there's a transistor radio underneath – which is not visually
satisfying, because you don't feel that this mechanism could have been
inside moving those facial features. So it started from the idea of doing
this sort of definitive movie robot, what I've always wanted to see.'

Cameron has a reputation as a director who is preoccupied with
technology but this mechanical skill is accompanied by a film fan's sense
of what the audience wants to be shown. He devoted scarcely any of his
limited resources to the time machine at the beginning of *The
Terminator*, because he rightly calculated that the audience would accept
that as a given. But since we are told so much about the cyborg's

capabilities, and then get to see it in action, we want to be shown the details of how it works.

The obvious influence of the psychopathic murderer in John Carpenter's highly successful *Halloween* (1978) is another example of Cameron's creative borrowing. Carpenter had based the entire structure of his film on the progress of an unstoppable killer, defying all traditions about character and suspense as to how he could be caught. The killer had no psychological motivation and was also, in some unexplained way, non-human, and apparently impossible to kill. As an abstract experiment in cinematic suspense it was interesting, as a cinematic narrative returns soon began to diminish.

A similar idea was used more compellingly the following year in the form of the lethal creature in Ridley Scott's *Alien* which slaughters

Westworld

the crew members of a spaceship one by one. The high-toned style of Kubrick's *2001* was applied to a B-picture plot featuring splattery violence that was previously more associated with exploitation movies.

In his first, unguarded days as a newly successful director, Cameron sprinkled his interviews with references to an extraordinary range of films which were not just vague stylistic influences, but sources of detail on which he could draw. Cameron was an open admirer of the pioneering action director Walter Hill: 'I had *The Driver* in mind when I was writing certain scenes in *The Terminator*. Not that I was cribbing; I had only seen the picture once and just had a dim memory of the kinetic forward energy.' And, presumably, the car-park interiors, the dark, deserted urban exteriors and the car chases. In due course, Hill himself became an admirer of *The Terminator* and tried to interest Cameron in a version of *Spartacus* set in space. Cameron was not interested in this, presumably because he had already used this as the inspiration for the character of John Connor, leading the human slaves in a revolt against the machines. Instead, Cameron agreed to write and direct the sequel to *Alien*. *The Driver* (1978) supplied the style of the modernday scenes, but for the glimpses of the future, Cameron had to look elsewhere: 'And then when I was writing *Terminator*, *The Road Warrior* came out and I said, "This is the next step." Nobody in between had come close.'

In *The Road Warrior* (1981; known in Australia and Britain as *Mad Max II*), George Miller created a brutal post-holocaust world, a tribalised society, almost pre-industrial in everything except its weaponry. It is sometimes forgotten that one of the innovations of *Star Wars* (1977) was that its futuristic technology was grimy and battered. George Miller and, in his wake, James Cameron took this further, giving the future the dirty, creaky look we associate with films set in the past. The World War II submarine in the war film Cameron so admired, *Das Boot* (1981), is not gleamingly solid but rattling, ricketty, leaking, dirty. Tech-Noir, the name of the nightclub in *The Terminator*, was also adopted as the name of Cameron and Hurd's production company, and it has frequently been cited as a description of Cameron's entire aesthetic. Whatever role

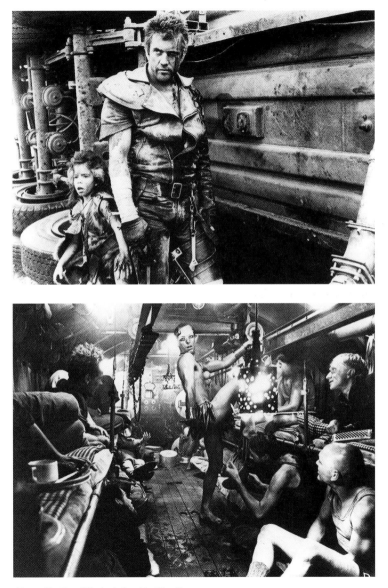

Above *The Road Warrior (a.k.a. Mad Max II)*
Below *Das Boot*

technology plays in Cameron's work, it is not the harbinger of a new, rational, efficient order. Like many of his generation, Cameron – who was born in 1954 – grew up watching *Star Trek* with its clean surfaces, its hygienic technology of phasers and transporter beams, and its jump-suited crew members. It was the suburban American kitchen projected into the future. By the time Cameron had begun to make films, the future had failed. For the first time in living memory, the standard of living of the American middle class was falling in real terms; there were social problems that couldn't be solved, diseases that couldn't be cured and the future of *Things to Come* (1936) no longer seemed convincing. The crew members of the Nostromo in *Alien* are grubby, pale, unshaven, unfit. They complain about their food and their wages.

In *Blade Runner* (1982), also directed by Ridley Scott, the rainy urban squalor of the future has apparently been left to the orientals, the latinos and to Harrison Ford. Scott's invention of the future was an awesome visual achievement, some compensation for the failures of the narrative. If budgetary constrictions prevented James Cameron from dwelling on the details of his invented future in the way the Scott did with long panning shots over futuristic urban scenes, then the loss of lyrical design in favour of narrative tautness was well worth it. Cameron may have been eclectic in his inspirations but he was never indulgent towards them. Directors like Brian De Palma, Joe Dante and John Landis seem unable to resist any allusion or visual joke that comes into their mind. This can be fun but when you are spotting a series of cameos by film directors in minor roles (in Landis's *Into the Night*) or spotting references to Hitchcock films (in many of De Palma's films), you can lose your involvement in the story. Cameron remains fully conscious of where his material comes from without ever winking at the cineastes in the audience. *The Terminator* is one of those films (John Sturges' *Bad Day at Black Rock* is another) which on a second viewing seems shorter than you expected. There are no distractions, no padding, no indulgence. The narrative's progress is as purposeful as that of the cyborg.

3 Making *The Terminator*

James Cameron is currently a beneficiary of the most lucrative production deal ever given to a movie director. Yet whatever freedom he is given, whatever power he goes on to achieve, he will never be able to recapture the creative opportunity he had when he made *The Terminator*.

He still had one foot in the raffish, small-scale Corman world of film-making in which the director could – had to – do a bit of everything. After the opening of the film, Cameron was conscious of the benefits of this method of working, even as he abandoned it for the opportunities and constraints of larger budgets. He said to *Film Comment*'s interviewer:

Terminator was in some ways an ultimate experience for me. I got to conceive the idea, write the script, have a deal made, storyboard the major scenes, go about creating those images in casting and sets and locations, then film it and compare the finished shots to the storyboard and see a satisfyingly similar type of image. For me it was a clean sweep. I got to do everything I wanted to do.

There was a minimum of actual interference from the movie's paymasters at Orion, partly because there was relatively little money at stake. There are only two recorded creative suggestions from the financiers. The first was the addition of a canine cyborg to accompany Reese, which Cameron turned down. The second was a strengthening of the love interest between Reese and Sarah, which Cameron willingly accepted. This resulted in the film's one period of repose, in the scenes in which the couple shelter first under the bridge and then in the motel, reminiscing, bandaging, making love and manufacturing explosives. Elsewhere, the necessary explanatory details are deftly incorporated into the action (unlike in the sequel, which is slowed down by a large number of expository sequences and lengthy dialogues).

Cameron was both knowledgeable about the possibilities of

special effects and financially limited in the number of them that he could use, so he was forced to decide which were the ones that really mattered. As Cameron later recalled in *Films and Filming,* 'Writing *Terminator* was really the art of throwing out and winnowing down, going on the basis of certain assumptions about the audience's education in science fiction.' What could he get away with omitting? The time travel at the beginning was suggested only by a few electric sparks that pleasingly recall the primitive technology of B science-fiction movies in the Flash Gordon tradition.

What could he get away with showing only in part? For much of the film, the mechanics of the cyborg are shown in carefully selected detail: the detachable eye into which Schwarzenegger plunges his scalpel, the creaking levers inside his damaged forearm.

What did the audience really need to see? Cameron husbanded his special effects resources for just two sequences with a shrewd sense of where they would be most needed. The first is the battle in the Los Angeles of 2029 seen at the beginning (and a few minutes later in Reese's memory), to give the audience an initial (and deftly misleading) impression of technical opulence. Even here, the computer forces are suggested with the utmost economy and because of the limited budget Cameron had to keep all these scenes brief and obliquely portrayed, with consequent benefits to the film's pace and structure. The second sequence was the appearance of the cyborg at the film's climax, burned down to its endo-skeleton. It emerges from the flames and chases Reese and Sarah into the factory.

Both these sequences were created by Fantasy II, a special effects company headed by Gene Warren Jnr. The second sequence involved cutting between two versions of the cyborg, a full-scale mechanical terminator constructed by the famous special effects man Stan Winston in his shop and a stop-motion puppet built by Doug Beswick at Fantasy II. The difficulties involved in the use of this model were considerable. Cameron insisted that the miniature had to be as detailed as the full-scale version, but financial limitations prevented the crew from building a smaller, more easily workable puppet. This puppet is seen nine times in full shot, walking out of the fire, moving down the corridor into the factory, on the catwalk and then, in the film's single most technically challenging sequence, receiving Reese's blow with a metal pipe.

Cameron storyboarded these episodes, but he knew that he wouldn't be able to supervise their production because of the pressure of time. Stan Winston's model wasn't completed until just before principal photography began and the puppet had to be constructed and filmed with almost no preliminary testing. Fortunately, Cameron's expertise extended also to a crucial understanding of what was unrealistic to demand of his technical crew. He wanted the cyborg's metal structure to convince the audience that it was capable of what the audience had seen Schwarzenegger doing, but it was evident that there

James Cameron

was no way that the stop-motion process could satisfactorily imitate Schwarzenegger's distinctive gait. So, in Schwarzenegger's final appearance on screen, we see him badly injured by the truck and limping away from it, a limp that the model could easily imitate. In the event, the animation was effective, and its occasional jerkiness could be excused, or even enjoyed, as a reminiscence of – even a homage to – Ray Harryhausen's celebrated stop-motion animation in films like *Jason and the Argonauts* and *One Million Years B.C.*

Cameron also benefited from low audience expectations, born of bitter experience of cheap SF movies. They didn't anticipate seeing much of how the cyborg actually worked in what was patently a low-budget film. Having startled and rewarded his audience in *The Terminator*, he would never be granted the luxury of low expectations again. In Cameron's later films the budgets would multiply drastically in constantly escalating attempts to startle the audience once more with the metamorphosing water creatures in *The Abyss*, the mimetic poly-alloy cyborg T1000 in *Terminator 2*, the helicopters and Harrier Jump Jet in *True Lies*. But that pleasure of surprise – the audience's delighted realisation that just for once it wasn't going to be ripped off – could never quite be recaptured.

4 The Plot

God, a person could go crazy thinking about this.
Sarah Connor, to her tape recorder.

Where does one start in summarising the story of *The Terminator*?
Numerous works of art make use of the idea of circularity. *Finnegans
Wake* and the fourth chapter of Nabokov's *The Gift* both finish by
leading the reader back to their beginning. The same is certainly true of
films like *Dead of Night*. A paradoxical form of circularity occurs in the
'Planet of the Apes' sequence of movies. In *Escape from the Planet of the
Apes*, the origin of talking apes on Earth is explained by a time travel
machine bringing two of them (Roddy McDowell and Kim Hunter) from
Earth's future.

But this is positively linear compared with the cumulative
developments in *The Terminator* and *Terminator 2*. Best perhaps to begin
in the middle, with Linda Hamilton's voiceover in the pre-credit
sequence of the sequel:

**Three billion human lives ended on August 29, 1997. The survivors of
the nuclear fire called the war Judgement Day. They lived only to
face a new nightmare: the war against the machines.**

**The computer which controlled the machines, Skynet, sent two
terminators back through time. Their mission, to destroy the leader
of the human resistance, John Connor, my son. The first terminator
was programmed to strike at me in the year 1984 before John was
born. It failed. The second was set to strike at John himself, when he
was still a child. As before, the resistance was able to send a lone
warrior, a protector for John. It was just a question of which one of
them would reach him first.**

The paradox in *The Terminator* is that the man sent back to protect
Sarah Connor actually fathers her child. John Connor knew that he was

sending his own father back in time in order that he himself be
conceived. In *Terminator 2* the paradoxes multiply. It emerges that the
sophisticated new technology which provoked the nuclear war was
developed from the fragments of the cyborg remaining in the factory at
the end of the first film. In *Terminator 2*, the cyborg not merely saves
John Connor but prevents the war which was responsible for sending
him back and thwarts the technological development which resulted in
himself being invented and then destroys himself in order to remove the
slightest possibility of himself being created. So by the end of
Terminator 2, the invention of the computer defence system, and hence
the nuclear war, has been forestalled. So the war with the computers will
never take place. So John Connor's heroic leadership of the men against
the machines will not be called for. So there will be no need to prevent

him being born, and no
terminator to do it even if
there was a need. So
there will be no need to
send Reese back to
protect the unborn John
Connor. So John Connor
won't be born. So in
which possible universe
have we ended up? It's
'tech stuff', as Reese
says.

By the end of
Terminator 2, the story is
not so much circular as a
spiral vanishing up its
own mimetic poly-alloy
fundament. Its enjoyably
baroque complications
(probably influenced by

Techno first aid

the playful paradoxes of Robert Zemeckis's 1985 time travel comedy, *Back to the Future*, in which, for example, Chuck Berry learns the riff of 'Johnny B. Goode' by hearing it played by Marty McFly, who learned it from listening to Chuck Berry) may obscure in retrospect the satisfying formal neatness of the first film. Reese has fallen in love with Sarah's photograph, given to him by her (and his) son, and he has always wondered what she was thinking about when it was taken. In the final moments of the film, as Sarah sits in a Mexican gas station telling her tape recorder about the love she and Reese shared in their brief hours together, a little boy takes a Polaroid photograph of her and sells it to her for four dollars. We see that it is Reese's photograph. Click. The circle of the story is complete. Sarah drives off into the impending nuclear holocaust and the audience walks out surprised and satisfied.

This efficiency of construction, a cross between *Star Trek* and O. Henry may seem a small thing, but it was a witty variation on the linear chase-and-kill structure of *Alien*, *Halloween* and even *Blade Runner*. When James Cameron came to make *The Terminator*, he had already established his credentials as a technician. The surprise was that he had applied his standards of craftsmanship to the story as well as to the special effects. In a Hollywood era in which the main plot twist comes when the villain/monster gets up again after the audience thinks it's dead, Cameron actually surprised the audience with some real plot twists. In his interview with *Film Comment* Cameron himself saw his achievement in typically technical terms: 'It was an underdog movie from a production standpoint. People come out of the theatre feeling that they got more than they expected from the marketing. That's positive word-of-mouth.'

5 Schwarzenegger

The first time Pauline Kael reviewed a James Cameron film (it was *Aliens* in August 1986), she described him as the man 'who directed the Schwarzenegger film *The Terminator*, and wrote the script for *Rambo: First Blood Part II* before Stallone reshaped it'.

And of course *The Terminator* is inescapably a Schwarzenegger picture, *the* Schwarzenegger picture, the film more than any other that turned him both into a cult and into a major international star. As Cameron himself admitted, the casting was crucial and altered the meaning of the film. The original plan had been to make, in Cameron's words, 'a gritty, street-level science-fiction movie that you would buy as if it was really happening.' He imagined the terminator as 'a more anonymous, saturnine figure' and the first actor he had in mind was Jürgen Prochnow, star of *Das Boot*. He was presumably intending a more down-at-heel version of the android-leader in *Blade Runner*, played by Rutger Hauer. Almost in reaction to *Blade Runner*, making a virtue once more of the budgetary limitations, *The Terminator* would have been a grim, punitive science-fiction tale, defined by Reese's austerity, the future existence of deprivation, pain and eternal conflict imported back into the 20th century. He might have been something like the T1000 model terminator (played by Robert Patrick), Schwarzenegger's antagonist in *Terminator 2*, when they certainly weren't going to cast an actor who would obliterate Schwarzenegger the way that Schwarzenegger obliterated poor Michael Biehn in *The Terminator*. Patrick is the cyborg as nerd, the cyborg as conformist company man, compared with Schwarzenegger who is bizarrely reincarnated in the sequel as a microchip representative of frontier independence.

Once Schwarzenegger was cast, the grim, realistic conception of the story was no longer tenable. In Cameron's words: 'With Arnold, the film took on a larger-than-life sheen. I just found myself on the set doing things I didn't think I would do – scenes that were supposed to be purely horrific that just couldn't be, because now they were too flamboyant.' This alteration was not due to any insight brought to the role by Schwarzenegger himself. Shrewd as he is, Schwarzenegger's analysis of his own work has generally been restricted to its importance for his long-term strategy in the industry. As he said early in his career in *Interview* (October 1985): 'I never think about money. I don't. I don't like that whole idea of being into money. I like to make good money only because it's part of the game. You have to have a certain value in Hollywood. There's the $5,000 actor, the $1 million actor, $5 million actor, and so on. You have a certain value, so you try to put yourself higher and higher up into this category.'

It has been said that Schwarzenegger was offered the part of Reese and opted for the part of the villain in order to broaden his range but this may well just be an attempt to give a retrospective

Schwarzenegger

purposefulness to what at the time must have seemed like the most routine of projects. According to Nigel Andrews' shrewd biography of the star, Schwarzenegger approached the film with little enthusiasm. Talking to a friend shortly before shooting started, he referred to it as 'some shit movie I'm doing, take a couple of weeks'.

Schwarzenegger's principal creative input in the years of his early success was to put more humour into his films in order to make his character more sympathetic. These resulted in the famous Arnie 'zingers', reminiscent of – and probably inspired by – the wisecracks in the James Bond films of Sean Connery and Roger Moore. Thus, in *Predator* (Schwarzenegger's best film apart from *The Terminator*) during a fight sequence, he throws a knife at a man, pinning him to a wooden post: 'Stick around,' he says, a remark which is entirely inappropriate for the sombre character Schwarzenegger was playing, but entirely suited to the persona he was developing. *Terminator 2* is full of these zingers, and we are even alerted to a hitherto unrevealed aspect of cyborg design which permits the development of human characteristics and hence allows Schwarzenegger to employ some of his – by then – trademark grimaces and narrowing of eyes, and to deliver carefully honed catchphrases: 'No problemo', 'Hasta la vista, baby.'

Schwarzenegger's mastery of self-invention and the management of his own career is not in doubt but Cameron knew how to use Schwarzenegger for his own purposes. Cameron is famous as a control freak, even in a profession of control freaks, and Schwarzenegger's only revealing memory of making *The Terminator* is an account of Cameron's direction of the scene when the terminator has been blasted through the windows of the Tech Noir club on to the Los Angeles sidewalk. Cameron stood to one side, off camera, and instructed him in every movement, from opening his eyes to the moment at which he should raise himself from the ground, as if he were another of Stan Winston's stop-motion models.

Cameron had caught Schwarzenegger at the right time and seen something in him. Sergio Leone once spoke of what had drawn him to cast a TV cowboy called Clint Eastwood in the leading role of *A Fistful of Dollars*: 'The story is told that when Michelangelo was asked what he had seen in one particular block of marble, which he had chosen among hundreds of others, he replied that he saw Moses. When they ask me what I saw in Clint Eastwood, I replied that what I saw, simply, was a block of marble.' James Cameron had had the same sort of perception. Schwarzenegger was 36 when he appeared in *The Terminator* and his career had already passed through several stages. In Bob Rafelson's undervalued *Stay Hungry* (1976) and George Butler and Robert Fiore's documentary *Pumping Iron* (1977) he had emerged as a bodybuilder with an unexpected charm and humour. *Conan the Barbarian* (1982) had made him well known but at the price of becoming the butt of the joke, a risibly cartoonish embodiment of John Milius's proto-samurai philosophy.

Conan the Barbarian

Schwarzenegger was poised for a career either in the straight-to-video market that seems to have claimed actors like Rutger Hauer and Dolph Lundgren (both more technically accomplished performers than Schwarzenegger) or in John Waters-style campery or perhaps the European muscleman epics of the kind that made Steve Reeves a cult. Cameron saw in this apparently absurd, overblown figure a poise and stillness that made apparent disqualifications, such as his accent and his inability to act, irrelevant.

Schwarzenegger's terminator demands to be compared with one of the mythic creations of the cinema, Boris Karloff's great performance as Frankenstein's monster in James Whale's 1931 film. The monster in Mary Shelley's novel was quite another thing, a person more sensitive and articulate than his creator. The original casting for the film was Bela Lugosi, who could only have been a small twisted maniac, more like Igor than the monster itself. But Lugosi turned the role down because of its lack of dialogue and Boris Karloff took it over. On the face of it, the film monster, with its metal bolts, its inhuman appearance, its criminal brain (stolen from the wrong jar) was a straightforward object of horror. But Karloff, huge and stately, lent the role his own gravity. Reaching for the light, attempting to play with a young girl, the creature became an embodiment not merely of pathos but of nobility. He defined the image of Frankenstein's monster for ever and the name of Boris Karloff became and remained one of the most famous in world cinema.

There are other points of resemblance between Karloff and Schwarzenegger. Both were immigrants who retained their foreign accents (Karloff was an English ex-public schoolboy). Both achieved fame relatively late (Karloff was 44 when he played the monster for the first time). Both were physically imposing, though Karloff developed his physique not in the gym but in the labouring jobs he did in the sizeable gaps between roles during the 1920s. But the differences between the two are more instructive about the Schwarzenegger phenomenon. Boris Karloff was an assumed name; Hollywood was not ready for a star called William Pratt. Arnold Schwarzenegger became the most famous star in the world, keeping a name that many of his fans couldn't spell or even pronounce. Yet it was Schwarzenegger who gleefully became an American citizen and married into the American royal family, the Kennedys. Karloff maintained his British citizenship, read *Wisden* and, from the mid-50s onwards, actually lived in England, leaving only to appear in films. Above all, the effect of Karloff's success in *Frankenstein* was to confine him to horror films for ever. How could an actor called Karloff do anything else? He played the Mummy and Fu Manchu and endless recyclings of Frankenstein's monster, and then with the decline of the horror genre in Hollywood, he went wherever they were made, however cheap and sleazy. He survived to benefit from the partial revival of the genre and appeared in two Roger Corman films (*The Raven* and *The Terror*, in 1962, both featuring the young Jack Nicholson). There

Boris Karloff

was never the smallest possibility that Karloff could use his fame to gain control over his films or to extend his range into other genres, as Schwarzenegger has done.

Schwarzenegger's terminator, who massacres a series of innocent bystanders, seems an unlikely object of the audience's admiration, let alone sympathy. Excluding the lines of dialogue in which Schwarzenegger is dubbed (such as when the terminator imitates Sarah Connor's mother over the telephone), he speaks seventy-four words of dialogue and kills twenty-seven people.

On the terminator's first appearance, the cyborg encounters three punks (their leader is played by Bill Paxton, who later played one of the marines in *Aliens*) and repeats what they say to him: 'Nice night for walk. ... Nothing clean ... right.' Then he adds: 'Your clothes. Give them to me now.' (Cameron's slightly off-key dialogue for the terminator complements Schwarzenegger's pronunciation, that idiosyncratic mixture of Austrian and southern Californian.)

Most of Schwarzenegger's long speeches take place in the gun shop where he acquires his armoury from the Corman repertory player Dick Miller. My transcript of the dialogue in this scene is unlikely to be accurate, but the word-count at least must be about right. The terminator asks for 'the twelve gauge autoloader, ... the .45 longslide with laser-sighting' and the as-yet-to-be-invented 'phased plasma rifle in a forty-watt range'. (Perhaps that's what the cyborgs are wielding in the first scene of *Terminator 2*.) The plasma rifle being unavailable, he settles for 'the Uzi nine millimetre'. Asked which of the weapons he wants, he replies, 'All.' Then, when cautioned that he isn't allowed to take them with him, he replies: 'Wrong.'

Knocking at the door of the first Sarah Connor, he says simply 'Sarah Connor' before shooting her in the head. Almost all of the rest of his dialogue is delivered at the beginning of the celebrated police station sequence. First he delivers his longest single speech of the film (though he is not required to manage it in a single take): 'I'm a friend of Sarah Connor. I was told that she's here. Can I see her please?' On being told that this is impossible he asks: 'Where is she?' Before leaving he delivers the line that was to become the first of his catchphrases: 'I'll be back.'

There is now almost half of the film remaining, fifty minutes, but Schwarzenegger speaks just ten more words. Back in his lodging house, the terminator's wounded flesh is starting to decay and the landlord inquires from outside the door whether he has a dead cat in his room: Schwarzenegger ripostes, with the film's best line, 'Fuck you, asshole.' After impersonating Sarah Connor's mother, the terminator calls the hotel: 'Give me your address there,' he demands. Finally, while commandeering the lorry, the immolation of which will burn his flesh away, the terminator speaks his final words of the film to the co-driver: 'Get out.'

As for the killings: the terminator kills the punk who draws a knife

In the gun shop

on him by plunging his fist into the young man's chest. This is the first, blackly comic touch of the film, and the first hint to the viewer that this character is not human. The second victim is the gun store salesman. The third victim is the first Sarah Connor, shot through the head just off camera. The fourth victim is the second Sarah Connor, whose murder

we only hear about. The fifth victim is Matt, the boyfriend of Sarah's
flatmate, Ginger, and the sixth is Ginger herself. Ginger's killing is the
most brutal in the film (the terminator's confusion of identity may have
been suggested by the similar mistake made by David Warner's Jack the
Ripper in Nicholas Meyer's 1979 *Time After Time*). Victims seven and
eight are bystanders in the Tech Noir club. Victims nine to twenty-five
are police officers (we are told in *Terminator 2* that seventeen police
officers were killed – if anything a suprisingly low figure). One mark of
the bracing unsentimentality, if not brutality, of the film is that by the
end of the film, most audience members have probably forgotten that
the terminator has killed not just the father of Sarah Connor's unborn
child, her best friend and the policemen who promised to protect her
but also her mother. She is the twenty-sixth victim with Reese as the
twenty-seventh and last. And this is the character who, according to
Cameron, had to be transformed into a hero in the sequel, because so
many young filmgoers admired him.

Cameron resists adding any humanising touches to the terminator.
Schwarzenegger himself observed in *Interview*, not entirely with
approval, that 'there was some indirect humour, but it wasn't written for
that; that was just the reaction of people'. The audience response to the
film revealed that there was something intrinsically attractive and comic
about Schwarzenegger, even in the grimmest of contexts. The murder of
Ginger, just after her energetic sex with Matt, is thoroughly in the genre
of those slasher movies in which sexually active women are butchered
one by one as some sort of psychopathic puritan revenge, and if the
terminator had been played by Jürgen Prochnow, it would have been
indistinguishable from similar scenes in films like *Halloween* or *He
Knows You're Alone*. But because it was Arnie, audiences half-knew that
it was all in fun.

Cameron claimed in *Film Comment* that Orion originally thought
that the poster of Schwarzenegger with his chest bared might attract
women to the film, 'but I don't think anyone sees him in a sexual way in
the film. They see him almost from the beginning as this implacable,

sexless, emotionless machine – in the form of a man, which is scary, because he's a perfect male figure.'

There was more than that. One of John Carpenter's much-copied innovations in *Halloween* was his sustained use of the Steadicam, a camera which could be strapped to a camera operator and could obtain tracking shots of a smoothness and a mobility that had previously been impossible. Carpenter saw that this mobile camera could be used to convey the stalking murderer's point of view, and he established this immediately with the virtuoso long opening shot of the film in which a camera prowls round a house before stabbing a naked woman to death. We then cut to the murderer, who turns out to be a small boy. This link between the voyeuristic murderer and the voyeuristic cinemagoer seated in the dark was a familiar enough theme, most obviously in the films of Alfred Hitchcock, but in the hands of Carpenter it became both powerfully insistent and coldly repellent. After all, it's not much fun, even in an irresponsible way, for moviegoers to identify with a man who stalks young girls and then stabs them to death.

But as Cameron was the first to see, the covert identification of the audience with the terminator really was fun. He realised from the beginning that the film allowed the audience to have it both ways. They want Reese and Sarah to get away, but they also have the chance to root for the bad guy (the following quotation, incidentally, is a further demonstration of the degree to which Cameron does most of the critics' work for them):

There's a little bit of the terminator in everybody. In our private fantasy world we'd all like to be able to walk in and shoot somebody we don't like, or to kick a door in instead of unlocking it; to be immune, and just to have our own way every minute. The terminator is the ultimate rude person. He operates completely outside all the built-in social constraints. It's a dark, cathartic fantasy. That's why people don't cringe in terror from the terminator but go with him. They want to be him for that one moment. But then when we go

back to Reese and Sarah, you get the other side of it, what it would be like to be on the receiving end.

This dark freedom was only possible because Cameron had still not entirely escaped from Corman's unrespectable exploitation world. The terminator's activities are unhampered not only by human morality but by directorial notions of decorum or good taste. Once the terminator slaughters the two Sarah Connors who come first in the Los Angeles phonebook and then Sarah's flatmate by mistake we can sit back in the pleasurable anticipation that he isn't going to turn sentimental on us. In the Tech Noir he shoots heedlessly into crowds and the glorious slapstick climax is reached in the police station which he rams with his car, shooting everybody on sight. In *Terminator 2* where this slaughter is recalled, we are piously informed that 'those men had families' but we didn't know that at the time, or want to know it.

The sequel shows what happens when James Cameron becomes self-conscious in a different way, assumes a civic mantle and forgoes the dark pleasure of being an exploitation director. The reprogrammed, reformed terminator of *Terminator 2*, whose powers are at the service of freedom, gives us none of that dark sense of release that we had in the first film. Instead, this large man with his access to Sarah Connor's secret cache of weapons is uncomfortably close to a survivalist with a righteous sense of mission. Admittedly there are a couple of grimly amusing murders committed by the T1000, most notably the almost casual dispatching of John Connor's stepfather with a blade through the head. This gives the opportunity for the best camera movement in the film, a tracking shot along the arm of the stepmother (whose shape the T1000 has assumed) as it becomes a blade penetrating first the carton of milk and then the stepfather's mouth. (The carton of milk is a sly reference to the murder of the senator in *The Manchurian Candidate*, shot by another dehumanised killer, the brainwashed Laurence Harvey, through a similar carton, causing him to 'bleed' milk.) But with his metamorphosing blades, the T1000 is too close to the psychopathic killer in a slasher movie for us to take much pleasure in it.

There is very little that could be described as a performance in Schwarzenegger's role as the terminator, yet experience shows that there is nothing as potent on the giant cinema screen as the blank face on to which the audience can project their fantasies and desires. Think of Garbo at the end of *Queen Christina* at the prow of the ship, famously instructed by Rouben Mamoulian to express nothing, to think of nothing, in the knowledge that the audience would do that for her. Clarence Brown, Garbo's most regular director, famously paid tribute to her impassivity: 'Garbo had something behind the eyes that you couldn't see until you photographed it in close-up. You could see thought. If she had to look at one person with jealousy, and another with love, she didn't have to change her expression. You could see it in her eyes as she looked from one to the other.'

In *The Terminator* Schwarzenegger took this even further. Not only does he lack expression in his eyes as well, he even slices one of them up in order to re-inforce the point. To a degree that even James Cameron could not have anticipated, Schwarzenegger demonstrated that the audience gravitates towards the character who has the aura of a hero and that impassivity is one of the crucial attributes of the film hero. Cary Grant was famous for wanting to give the lines in the bread-and-butter expository scenes that give the audience essential but non-dramatic information to supporting actors while he would do what stars do best, which is to listen.

The Terminator spectacularly succeeded in making Arnold Schwarzenegger a star. It spectacularly failed to make stars of the ostensible heroes of the film, Michael Biehn and Linda Hamilton. In the improbable event that we encountered Biehn's Reese in real life, we would consider him to be an extraordinary hero. He sacrifices himself for a mission to save a woman, out of idealism but also because he has fallen in love with her picture (like Tamino in Mozart's *Magic Flute*). He arrives in our world with nothing and manages to save Sarah Connor with the pitiful weapons available to him and, more than this, to awaken her to her true self. But heroism doesn't work like that on the big screen. It has been noted before that since Schwarzenegger's terminator isn't going to explain to us who he is and what he's doing there and how he got there and what life is like in the future and why the computers are fighting against the humans, then Michael Biehn will have to do it and that leaves him with an awful lot of explaining to do. There is remarkably little dialogue in the intriguing, mysterious early scenes of *The Terminator* as Cameron cleverly keeps the audience wondering about who these two men are. Then things suddenly get garrulous as Reese has to explain to Sarah that Schwarzenegger is 'a cyborg, a machine, a terminator, Cyberdyne systems model one zero one. Infiltration unit. Underneath it's a hyper-alloy combat chassis. Microprocessor controlled, fully armoured. Very tough. But outside it's living human tisue. The 600 series had rubber skin. Easy to spot.' And so on.

Once Reese is under detention, the true Hollywood hero would

Reese in custody

stay contemptuously silent, but Reese still has information to impart to the audience. The unfortunate result is that we see him blabbing away to the police like a stoolie. When he is asked about how he will get back, he stoically replies, 'Nobody goes back, nobody else goes through. It's just him and me.' But even this heroism leaves us uncomfortable. He ought to have a sidekick, a Walter Brennan, who can tell us all about that. Cinematic heroes aren't meant to bleat about their own heroism. They just do it. The reason that Humphrey Bogart can be so laconic and modest in *Casablanca* is that Claude Rains, Conrad Veidt, Sydney Greenstreet, Paul Henreid and almost everybody else keep informing him about his own heroism and idealism.

And while Reese is identifying himself as a soldier from the 132nd under Parry, and describing the enemy, a computer defence system built for SACNORAD by Cyberdyne systems and about Skynet and about time displacement equipment and explaining why it is too late for the enemy to kill John Connor in their own time, the terminator is striding into the police station and just saying: 'I'll be back.'

Biehn's very capability as an actor, in obvious contrast to Schwarzenegger, is part of his problem and this was only compounded by the scenes, extended on the advice of the film's producers, in which Reese's relationship with Sarah was emphasised. Reese talks of the brutality of life in the future, of the pain of travelling through time and the love for Sarah that has brought him here: 'So much pain,' Sarah says, stroking him. These complicated emotions which should make him more sympathetic actually make him seem weak and neurotic. Pursuing a woman across time, which might seem impressive in a narrative poem or a novel, appears on the big screen more like the behaviour of a stalker. Reese's most impressive achievement of all, galvanising Sarah into discovering and developing her inner resources, counts against him as well. The first sign of Sarah's strength, when she bandages Reese's wound under the bridge, is acceptable. The hero is permitted to be nursed by the woman he loves. But after the final car chase, when Reese has been badly wounded, when he collapses and is ordered to his feet by Sarah, he is failing in his duty as a hero. Worst of all, an authentic action movie hero does not die and leave the heroine to face the villain alone, however capable she may be. Compare the climax of *Terminator 2* in which the terminator, minus an arm and much of his head, appears at the crucial moment to blast the T1000 into the vat of molten metal.

There is a substantial problem with this explanation. In *Terminator 2* Arnold Schwarzenegger takes the Michael Biehn role, while Robert Patrick takes the strong, silent Schwarzenegger role. This time it's Arnie who has to embark on the long explanations about the mimetic poly-alloy and why the T1000 can't just turn into a bomb and blow John Connor up. Then he must explain to Linda Hamilton about the details of Cyberdine's part in the development of computer technology. According to the pattern demonstrated in the audience's response to the first film, viewers should have started rooting for Robert Patrick's T1000. Why didn't they?

Arnie was now a world famous star and had to be protected, so he and Cameron made sure he wasn't upstaged. The same kinds of dry technical explanation are more acceptable from the terminator because he is a computer and are actually a sign of his imperturbability and strength. They can also have a laconic power of their own, such as when the terminator imitates John in a phonecall to his fosterparents and then replaces the receiver with the dry statement: 'Your fosterparents are dead.' The reprogrammed terminator is cleverly portrayed as an ideal father-figure for John (yet another insult to the defunct Reese) and when he first saves the boy from the T1000, he doesn't just jump out of the way of the bullets, he does what every father would like to do, he interposes his body, taking the other terminator's bullets in his own back. And in case we happen to have missed the point, Cameron spells it out for us in the form of Sarah's thoughts spoken in a voiceover:

Watching John with the machine, it was suddenly so clear. The terminator would never stop, it would never leave him and it would never hurt him, never shout at him or get drunk and hit him or say it was too busy to spend time with him. It would always be there and it would die to protect him. Of all the would-be fathers who came and went over the years, this thing, this machine was the only one who measured up. In an insane world it was the sane choice.

When Reese informs Sarah that the terminator can't be bargained with, can't be reasoned with, he sounds like a whiner. By contrast, when the terminator dispassionately informs John of the superior capabilities of the T1000 he makes himself sound like an underdog we want to cheer.

Great pains were evidently taken to ensure that no misplaced sympathy went the way of the T1000. Dressing him throughout in a purloined police uniform makes him seem cowardly (the police are at best hapless onlookers in all James Cameron's work). He is neither strong and silent, nor is he given anything to say that could conceivably become a catchphrase. Instead, he is only given geekish dialogue like, 'Say, that's a nice bike.' He's given feeble pistols to fire as well, always a sign of moral inadequacy in the world of James Cameron. The T1000

'So much pain',
Sarah says

could never become a cult hero, except to other geeks and stalkers and anorak wearers.

The main difference, though, between Arnold Schwarzenegger and Michael Biehn (let alone Robert Patrick) is that Schwarzenegger is a star in a way that Biehn could never hope to be. As the terminator, Schwarzenegger has that quality that Ronald Reagan had as President of the United States on state occasions, that occasional hint of the twinkle in the eye, the half smile, that showed his own recognition of the improbability of what had happened, and that he was enjoying it and therefore we were free to enjoy it too. Michael Biehn's skilled performance gives us the feeling of the pain of being a hero, of self-sacrifice, the fear of failure, of disaster. Arnold Schwarzenegger makes us feel the enjoyment of watching a film, of guns and explosions and violence, all in the knowledge that he doesn't really mean it and that the lights will come up and we can all go home.

Yet there are limits, even to charm of this magnitude. The one-liners in *Terminator 2* are amusing, but they begin to pall during its excessive length (more than half an hour longer than *The Terminator*) and in later films, like *Last Action Hero* and *Junior*, Schwarzenegger's self-deprecating humor slackened the grip of the narrative to the extent that both films lost their audience.

The Terminator is Arnold Schwarzenegger's great cinematic moment. In later films he displays the practised ease of a politician on the campaign trail, but it is only here that all his attributes, from the slightly dislocated oddness of his accent to the chiselled physiognomy and the inflated physique, all work for the film. In *The Terminator* he did what he could do; his success in the role enabled him to devote himself to what he can't do.

6 Defending *The Terminator*

The Terminator is so viscerally enjoyable an experience, so deftly crafted, so unexpectedly satisfying in its resolution, that there is the temptation to legitimise this pleasure by demonstrating that the film is good for you as well, that it is 'really' a serious work, with grown-up ideas, respectable themes and a basically liberal political vision. And here, as elsewhere, Cameron provides his audience with the material to work on. As he put it, speaking to *Film Comment* shortly after the film's first success:

The producer, Gale Hurd, and I set out to make a movie that would function on a couple of levels: as a linear action piece that a 12-year-old would think was the most *rad* picture he'd ever seen, and as science fiction that a 45-year-old Stanford English prof would think had some sort of socio-political significance between the lines – although obviously it doesn't attempt to be that primarily.

What might this imaginary middle-aged Stanford English professor say about the film in the campus coffee shop after the screening? She might point out that the film is a feminist subversion of what had been a quintessentially male genre, and that Cameron, with his collaborator (and, briefly, wife), Gale Anne Hurd, would go on to re-inforce this in a series of high-tech action pictures. We first encounter Sarah Connor as a down-trodden, but good-humoured waitress, with her wise-cracking colleague and flatmate, Ginger. It's a standard, complacent sitcom setting, and this is followed by a series of other disparaging images of Sarah: she is the fun-loving but basically unreflective party animal. She is not merely going out with empty-headed men who drive Porsches; they stand her up on Friday night. She is a helpless victim of the terminator, saved by luck and the repeated intervention of her male rescuer. But then she finds her hidden resources first in nurturing Reese ('Good field dressing,' he compliments her), learning from him about explosives and finally becoming the active partner and destroying the terminator herself.

Better still, she allows Reese to display his feminine, emotional, neutrotic side, deconstructing the traditional model of icy heroism and dismantling Michael Biehn's career as a leading man in the process. The perfect image of male heroism in the film is a robot, and it is the woman who survives, triumphant, pregnant and alone.

Cameron's predilection for strong women continued in his later films. His sequel to *Alien* made the strength of Sigourney Weaver's Ripley the centre of the film. Her instinct for survival, and that of the little girl, Newt, exposes the superficiality of the military ethic. All of his films, *Aliens*, *The Abyss*, *Terminator 2*, *True Lies*, feature weak, neurotic men and strong women.

The Stanford professor might add that *The Terminator* is also 'rad' in a different sense. It is anti-establishment, distrusting the traditional paternalistic role of the police. It is anti-capitalist; it is made clear that the disastrous nuclear annihilation was the result of a collaboration between big government and big business. And the name given to the defence system, Skynet, is an obvious reference to the Star Wars system and the destabilising effects even of military projects that are ostensibly defensive. The film is pro-gun control. The terminator is able to arm himself with an awesome array of firepower directly off the shelf, provoking one of the script's moments of dry humour. The scene exposes the absurdity of such half-measures as the fifteen-day wait on buying a handgun, when machine-guns can be carried away immediately.

Furthermore, the defender might add, the film eschews the usual blind adoration for technology that is traditionally at the heart of the science fiction genre. In this story of a planet almost destroyed by the overweening power of its technological development, one of the recurrent themes is the fallibility of technology at every level. The nuclear war began because the defence network became conscious (at 2.14 a.m. Eastern Time on 29 August 1997) and began to defend itself. In smaller ways, throughout the film, we see that our machines never seem to work as they should. Phones are broken, and even when Sarah Connor gets through to the police she is put on hold. The entire telephone system as a means of communication is presented as fatally corrupted. When Matt rings Ginger with a cod obscene phone-call he speaks to Sarah instead, a mistake that is tragically repeated when the terminator imitates Sarah's mother over the phone to Sarah in the motel. Sarah's answering machine is the vehicle first for being stood up by her date and then for alerting the terminator that Sarah Connor is still alive and in hiding at the Tech Noir nightclub. Even the phonebook becomes the tool of a murderer. Ginger's personal stereo is partly responsible for her death: it prevents her from hearing the terminator in her apartment.

Some literary professors might even argue that *The Terminator* is a serious work of art because of its religious theme. John Connor shares his initials with that other redeemer of mankind, Jesus Christ, and the

The telephone system is fatally corrupted

film is an obvious allegorical conflation of the Nativity with the story of Eve and the serpent. Reese is a version of the annunciatory angel who impregnates Mary as well as informing her of the glad tidings. The terminator is a Herod, slaughtering the Sarah Connors instead of the first born, and he is also a Satan, who by attempting to destroy humanity perversely brings about its salvation (the paradoxical story Milton tells in *Paradise Lost*). So *The Terminator* must be serious, mustn't it?

But *The Terminator* resists being made comfortable and reassuring. Its politics are darker and more ambiguous than such well-intentioned but misguided defences suggests. There is a tendency, especially viewed from a misleading British context, to interpret a distrust of the police and the military as necessarily left wing. But in the United States there is a quite separate right-wing anti-authoritarian tradition, an individualism which sees almost all forms of social organisation and control – police, army, federal government, tax collection, even printed money – as creeping forms of communism which are neutering the pioneering spirit that built America. This conviction can move beyond political belief to become a pathological psychological condition, one that Richard Hofstadter famously labelled 'the paranoid style in American politics' in his celebrated book of that name. The darkest expression of this was seen in the Oklahoma City bombings, first thought to be the work of foreign terrorists, then discovered to be the product of a right-wing subculture which considers itself to be at war with the American government on behalf of the true spirit of America.

The law enforcement officers in *The Terminator*, as well as the ordinary people they serve, have become weak and incapable of defending their own way of life, which is itself alienated and parasitic (as with Sarah's flatmate, Ginger, who even listens to her personal stereo during sex). In the face of the nuclear threat and the challenges of technological change, individuals are relinquishing the responsibility for their own future. Cameron admitted to being dismayed by interviews with high school kids after the TV screening of the nuclear drama, *The Day After*, who said that they now accepted nuclear war as inevitable:

In *The Terminator* the fact of nuclear war is thrown away, with the complete understanding that people will buy it. It's just part of the fabric of the story. On the other hand, it tried to say that you take responsibility for your own life, and for the life of society. The terminator looks like death, and if you want to read into it, it's a death image. Linda Hamilton's character faces that image of death, or fate, and survives.

All that has resonance, I hope, with the dark premonitory character of Reese's future-flashbacks, as I call them, and with the final image of driving off into a storm. It's fate vs. will.

Cameron's fable of a disastrous breakdown in society, a future conflict in which success will depend on the individual's will, bolstered by years of training and a personal armoury, owes more to survivalism than to socialism. Sarah Connor's defeat of the terminator is a Nietzschean assertion of superiority. She survives because she has fought for her right to rule, unlike the other Sarah Connors and the enfeebled police force. Far from being a representative of any recognisable form of feminism, Sarah is the embodiment of something stranger and more primitive, the woman defending her child, the tigress fighting to defend her cub, which is also the future of mankind. It could be argued that even Sarah Connor has been corrupted by her life as a working woman and a fun-seeking sexual adventuress. She only becomes a match for the terminator when she has been impregnated by Reese and placed in touch with a more ancient femaleness. Once she has become a mother (and the pro-choice lobby would presumably claim that she has become a mother at the moment of conception), she is able to fight.

Pro-gun control? In the consciously mythic final sequence, before Sarah drives off on a road to somewhere that is half-Bethlehem, half-Armageddon, we see her bright, silver handgun nestling on her lap against her rounded pregnant stomach, soft and hard, rounded and phallic, nurturer and killer, brought together in an image that would be appropriate for a portrait of the Madonna in the chapel at the headquarters of the National Rifle Association.

These matters could remain richly inchoate in *The Terminator* but for the sequel, where the budget was so much higher, the politics had to be made clearly balanced and acceptable. Cameron was a Hollywood insider by now, and the once dark issues are brought into the light and urbanely defused and satirised. Rather than buy his weapons from a gun shop, the newly programmed terminator avails himself of Sarah Connor's secret arms cache in the hispanicised south of California. 'Excellent,' the terminator comments on seeing the ranks of machine-guns. This might seem dangerously like a legitimisation of crackpot survivalism, but Cameron permits us to laugh at the excessiveness of it all. Schwarzenegger picks up a ridiculously large machine-gun. 'That's definitely you,' comments little John Connor. Later in the film, the script itself anxiously makes the feminist point that the Stanford professor

Linda Hamilton in
Terminator 2

might have inferred from the first film, as Sarah Connor attacks a male scientist, and all males scientists, for creating the bomb and all those other technological horrors, when they are unable to perform the true creative act of making a baby. The feminist point is made, but also undercut as we are shown that she is ranting, and as her son calls on her to be more constructive. Is it pro-feminist with a sense of humour? Is it exposing feminist cant? Whatever. And that's the way it's meant to be.

Terminator 2 is a nice film in which everybody is saved, including Jesus, as, in a last-minute alteration to the story, the father lays down his life so that the son doesn't have to suffer after all. But The Terminator retains its uncomfortable darkness, as unrelenting as the detached arm and torso of the smashed terminator, dragging itself after Sarah. We want what we like to be light and bright and civic-minded like Terminator 2, so why is it that The Terminator stays with us? William Hazlitt explored this unsettling issue in his great essay on Coriolanus (first published in 1816). For poetry read cinema:

The cause of the people is indeed but little calculated as a subject for poetry: it admits of rhetoric, which goes into argument and explanation, but it presents no immediate or distinct images to the mind, 'no jutting frieze, buttress, or coigne of vantage' for poetry 'to make its pendant bed and procreant cradle in.' The language of poetry naturally falls in with the language of power. The imagination is an exaggerating and exclusive faculty: it takes from one thing to add to another: it accumulates circumstances together to give the greatest possible effect to a favourite object. The understanding is a dividing and measuring faculty: it judges of things not according to their immediate impression on the mind, but according to their relations to one another. The one is a monopolising faculty, which seeks the greatest quantity of ultimate good, by justice and proportion. The one is an aristocratical, the other a republican faculty. The principle of poetry is a very anti-levelling principle. It aims at effect, it exists by contrast. It admits of no medium.

**It is every thing by excess. It rises above the ordinary standard of
sufferings and crimes. It presents a dazzling appearance. It shows
its head turretted, crowned, and crested. Its front is gilt and blood-
stained. Before it 'it carries noise, and behind it leaves tears.' It has
its altars and its victims, sacrifices, human sacrifices. Kings, priests,
nobles, are its train-bearers, tyrants and slaves its executioners. –
'Carnage is its daughter.' – Poetry is right-royal. It puts the individual
for the species, the one above the infinite many, might before right.
A lion hunting a flock of sheep or a herd of wild asses is a more
poetical object than they; and we even take part with the lordly beast,
because our vanity or some other feeling makes us disposed to place
ourselves in the situation of the strongest party. . . . We had rather be
the oppressor than the oppressed. The love of power in ourselves
and the admiration of it in others are both natural to man: the one
makes him a tyrant, the other a slave. Wrong dressed out in pride,
pomp, and circumstance, has more attraction than abstract right.**

When Judy Garland says goodbye to Bert Lahr at the end of *The
Wizard of Oz*, she admits that she misses the way he behaved when he
was terrified. The reprogrammed terminator of the sequel who doesn't
kill people and dies to save humanity may be sweet, but any honest
filmgoer preferred the homicidal cyborg who murdered women and
policemen. This apparent perversity of response is one of the dark
pleasures of filmgoing, in which we respond to vitality rather than
morality. It's why we nice people enjoy watching Jimmy Cagney slam a
grapefruit into Mae Clarke's face in *Public Enemy*, a film that paraded
itself as an indictment of gangsterism. But when the brilliance of Malcolm
McDowell's performance, and our emotional distancing from his victims,
makes us enjoy the beatings and rapings of *A Clockwork Orange*, it is time
to start worrying. But worrying about what? Stanley Kubrick? The whole
irresponsible potency of the cinematic image? Ourselves?

As for the film's religious allegory, it should be remembered that
John Connor shares his initials with James Cameron as well as Jesus
Christ.

7 Watching *The Terminator*

The first hour of *The Terminator* divides into twenty-five scenes. With the imaginary Stanford professor replaced by a notional first-time viewer, the effect might be something like this.

1. The Los Angeles 2029 caption is seen over a desolate, post-holocaust landscape, an amusing enough visual joke. We see some flying ships shooting ray guns, isolated skirmishes, in a sequence that was not, incidentally, directed by James Cameron. The special effects are nothing startling, even for 1984, but we're mildly curious. There is an introductory text. We don't usually pay much attention to these clotted explanations of why King John happens be on the throne or why we are in a galaxy long ago and far away, but the statement that the war will be fought 'not in the future but our present. Tonight' is a surprise.

The credits. There's nobody we've heard of except for that Schwarzenegger person who was in *Conan the Barbarian*. What's a terminator?

2. Back in the future, no, it's the present. A truck is lifting garbage. A dull few seconds and then some flashes of electricity. A naked man standing up. A muscleman. Is this a gay film? He looks purposeful and walks forward to look out across Los Angeles. Now he encounters some punks and demands their clothes. A great scene, grisly and horribly funny. The sudden extra violence makes us wonder who this man is. We're sitting up now. It's starting to look good.

3. A police siren, an alley, another naked man. Smaller. He's hurt, smoking. Are they together? He is chased by the police along small streets. By now we've guesssed that the two men are from the future world we saw at the beginning. What are they up to? He grabs a rifle from an unattended police car. This is promising. How are the two men

going to meet up with each other? He rips a page out of the phonebook with the name Sarah Connor.

4. Linda Hamilton, with a B-movie hairstyle, on a motorscooter. Arriving at a burger restaurant, she clocks in as Sarah Connor.

5. The big man breaks into a car, punching the window out with his hand. This is more like it.

6. Some rather tired sitcom-style harassment of Sarah in the burger bar. She spills a drink over a customer and a boy slips an ice cream into her apron. Is there a point to this? It seems a little second-rate.

7. The big man enters a gun shop. This is another great scene, as he acquires a preposterously large armoury. What can he want all that for? Dick Miller's lines are snappy and there is the sudden killing at the end.

8. The other man saws the barrel off his single rifle. What's he up to?

9. The big man, looking for a phonebook, tugs another large man away from it without even looking at him. From off-screen: 'Hey, man, you've got a serious attitude problem.' We're starting to enjoy the Schwarzenegger scenes. He's looking for Sarah Connor.

10. A car drives over a toy truck in a suburban street. Schwarzenegger approaches the front door of a house and asks for Sarah Connor. Is he really going to kill this ordinary-looking woman? Yes.

11. Taking a break at work, Sarah is shown the item on the news.

12. Reese is stealing a car next to a construction site. Flash-forward to a battle with the Skynet craft. Reese is one of the combatants. The sequence is exciting, brutal. This is no sanitised view of future warfare.

Almost everybody is killed. He wakes up back at the building site and drives away.

13. Sarah is in her apartment with her friend Ginger, getting ready to go out. The silly joke about Matt's dirty phone-call to the wrong woman. A poorly acted, overstated scene.

14. Our first view of the police detectives, who seem sleazy and incompetent. We are taken by surprise by hearing about the *second* Sarah Connor murder. This is getting exciting.

15. Back to the apartment where Sarah has been stood up. Why is this airhead so important? She heads out to a movie on her own. She's being followed by Reese.

16. The police again and the press. The murders followed the listing in the phonebook. Our Sarah is next on the list. Aren't the police going to protect her? They prove incapable even of contacting her. The police chief is drinking bad coffee, smoking, taking pills. They phone her apartment but Ginger is in bed with Matt and they don't answer.

17. Sarah sees the news on TV in a pizza restaurant. The phone doesn't work. She walks out and, noticing that she's being followed, ducks into the Tech Noir and Reese walks past. She phones the police. All the lines are busy.

18. Arnie is approaching the apartment building. We've seen our share of slasher movies and we know what's going to happen. After killing Ginger, Arnie hears the answering machine: it's Sarah, giving away her location. There's going to be a showdown.

19. Sarah has finally got through to the police. They tell her to stay where she is, that she'll be safe. She puts the phone down and Arnie

arrives at the club immediately. An exciting gun battle, culminating in Reese blasting Arnie through the window. He gets up unhurt. Is this just going to be another *Halloween* rip-off? Reese reaches his hand out to Sarah and says simply: 'Come with me if you want to live.' Reese and Sarah escape down an alley. Arnie jumps on their car and punches through the windscreen. They throw him off and become involved in a car chase, while Reese shouts out an explanation about the terminator, who has purloined a police car. We know what sort of film we're in now. After a chase in a car-park, Reese and Sarah are caught by the police and the terminator is nowhere to be seen.

20. We're in the police station. Are we safe for a while? Sarah meets an absurd movie psychiatrist.

21. The terminator is climbing into his room. His face is damaged, his hand paralysed. Badly injured, he reaches for a scalpel and slices into his arm. We aren't cheated, we get to see the pullies and levers. The hand is working once more.

22. Reese is interrogated by the psychiatrist who asks the questions we've been wanting to ask, about why he didn't bring ray guns along and all that stuff.

23. The terminator turns his attention to his wrecked eye. He grabs the scalpel, to anticipatory groans from the audience. Is he really going to? Are we going to see it? He is. We are. He plunges it all the way in. We're not spared anything. He puts on sunglasses (the manufacturer's name on the frame is Gargoyle). He picks up two large guns. He's not going to storm the police station, is he?

24. Back to Reese's interrogation, which is being viewed on a video now, by the police, Sarah and the psychiatrist. Reese says that the terminator will find her. That's what he does. Nobody can stop him. The detective

lies her down on his couch, covers her with his jacket and tells her that she is safe. After all, what could happen to her in a police station?

25. The greatest scene in the film. The psychiatrist leaves the station and takes us by surprise by passing the terminator who is on his way in. (An example of Cameron's ruthless sense of humour: the one character that we would actively like to see get blasted, the psychiatrist, escapes by pure chance.) Then the terminator delivers the classic 'I'll be back' line. The long pause after he has gone may remind us of the moments in *Jaws* when we are waiting for something terrible to happen. What is the terminator going to do? Then the car crashes through. Can this really be happening? He wanders through the police station blasting policeman after policeman. In Cameron's words, recalling the two great set-pieces in *Films and Filming*:

Ah, the disco, the police station and all that – they clearly reflect a warped childhood! Maybe it's because I got a lot of speeding tickets when I was a kid – it's my catharsis. … It's not intended to make some grand statement about a police state or whatever. But it may relate to the idea of the terminator in all of us, and the fact that some people allow the machine to take over a little too much and that's what makes them boring bureaucrats or officious little police officers. So when Arnold comes into the police station there's an irony there that tickled me as I wrote it.

It's a glorious slapstick sequence, that makes you laugh because of its excess and flamboyance and lack of shame. Are we really allowed to enjoy all these cops getting blown away? Reese and Sarah sneak out the back and escape in a stolen car. The terminator shoots at them but they get away. The screen fades slowly to black and we slump in our seats a little. Exactly an hour of the film has passed, and it is our first chance to pause for breath.

Even a summary of these scenes gives a flavour of the film's momentum which is increased by suddenly dragging us forward more quickly than we expect. From the murder of the first Sarah Connor straight to Sarah watching the report of it on the news. The police reacting to the two Sarah Connor killings when we didn't know the second one had occurred. And Cameron gives us a start by impossibly but effectively telescoping the time scheme of events as the terminator catches up with Sarah. For example: he hears Sarah's voice on the telephone answering machine warning Ginger, saying she is at the Tech Noir and that she will phone the police again. Cut to Sarah talking to the detective who tells her to stay put and that a police car is on its way. (Who will get there first, the police or the terminator?) Cut to the terminator entering the Tech Noir.

In the Tech Noir

The summary also demonstrates Schwarzenegger's dominance of the film. Cameron rightly observed that it was a film that took audiences pleasurably by surprise. It was better than they had expected and its reputation quickly spread by word of mouth, the best advertising a film can have. Of the first twenty-five scenes, there are seven really good ones, of the kind that you might tell people about afterwards, and they all feature Schwarzenegger: the encounter with the punks, the gun shop, pulling the man out of the phone booth, the gun battle in the Tech Noir, the auto-surgery on the arm and the eye, and the battle at the police station. They are all, in their different ways, funny. Sometimes the humour arises from other characters – Dick Miller in the gun shop, the big man telling the terminator he has an attitude problem – but we laugh because of Schwarzenegger's impassivity. One of the best comic tactics in cinema is that of letting things happen around you. Oliver Hardy did it, and so did Cary Grant. By contrast, nobody laughs much at the tired jokes about the police psychiatrist or Sarah's pet reptile.

The dullest scenes are those involving Sarah, but this serves the story equally well. We feel we ought to be scared on her behalf, and we are a bit, but we also want to see the terminator again and we also think she's better off being driven out of her vapid daily existence. Like Cameron's other screen heroines, Sarah Connor only becomes chic when she is in combat gear and carrying a gun.

Most of what people remember about *The Terminator* comes from this first hour of the film. What remains is more conventional, and Cameron's principal challenge was to sustain the extraordinary excitement he had created. To the extent that he succeeds, it is because of his remarkable economy of means. The rest of the film consists of what are in effect three sequences: the interlude between Sarah and Kyle; the long chase culminating in the factory, and the highly effective kicker featuring Sarah in the Mexican gas station where we learn how Reese's photograph of her was taken. This second half is more routine than the first, yet it is when the film is at its most formulaic, in the final chase in the factory, that Cameron can show his trump card: Stan Winston's brilliant model of the cyborg's endoskeleton. This model is both terrifying and comic, with its dead man's grin. Just at the moment when the film is starting to seem cheap, Cameron shows us the only expensive special effect he had.

8 Afterlife

The absence of a major publicity campaign accompanying the release
of *The Terminator* was itself an advantage because there was no hype
which critics and filmgoers felt impelled to resist. Despite having been
immediately acclaimed and having become a commercial success, it had
the air of a B-picture underdog, of a cult film. Audiences felt they were
discovering it for themselves. It was a meeting of minds between the
film-maker and his audience. James Cameron had known what he was
doing. Audiences recognised what he had done and applauded him for
it. Dan Scapperotti, reviewing the film in the May 1985 issue of the
American SF film magazine *Cinefantastique,* spoke for almost everybody
when he hailed a film that 'manages to be both derivative and original at
the same time' and rejoiced that 'not since *Road Warrior* has the genre
exhibited so much exuberant carnage'. He concluded with perfect
foresight:

**The Terminator is an example of science fiction/horror at its best,
intelligently integrating today's high tech special effects with a
viable, frightening story. Cameron's no-nonsense approach will make
him a sought-after commodity in an industry that has discovered big
bucks in this type of entertainment.**

The parodic, schlock movie critic from Dallas, Joe Bob Briggs,
hailed the film ecstatically: 'We're talking drive-in heaven.' The film was
taken seriously as well. *Time* magazine selected it as one of the ten best
films of 1984, describing it as 'the smartest looking LA night town movie
since *The Driver*'. The reception in Britain the following year was equally
favourable. Julian Petley's review in *Monthly Film Bulletin* began:

**Not to be confused with the Exterminator series, which is made to
seem very small beer indeed, The Terminator announces itself as a
delirious, rip-roaring, all-stops-out mating of Mad Max 2 and Blade**

Runner: a union which grafts the tremendous momentum of the former on to the elaborate *mise en scène* of the latter.

Petley praised the film's script, special effects, design and the performance of Schwarzenegger. He offered no criticisms at all.

The film was also lucky in being released at a time when it could benefit from the newly burgeoning video market. In video rentals for 1985, the film was second only to *Karate Kid*.

The Terminator's reputation has remained high. It was scarcely controversial, for example, when *Esquire* magazine selected it as 'the film of the eighties'. Apart from the film's obvious qualities, for which it had been widely praised, the film's longevity was aided once more by the budgetary limitations under which Cameron had been working. He had been forced to suggest the futuristic world, rather than show us its imagined technology in detail, and even the brilliantly realised cyborg itself was only shown to us in glimpses. There were few of the then state-of-the-art computer graphics that date so quickly (the graphics seen on the computer screens in *2001* and *Alien* are good examples of what now seem amusingly primitive).

Cameron was immediately questioned about the possibility of a sequel. He responded pessimistically because by then he had fallen out badly with the producers who owned the rights. But as Cameron and Schwarzenegger both became major forces in the film industry, the idea became commercially irresistible and it became possible once more when Cameron was able to buy the rights back.

Terminator 2: Judgment Day is a story in itself. By contrast with its predecessor, it made use of innovative but highly costly special effects. Yet, against many expectations, it showed that a film costing more than twice as much as *Heaven's Gate* could be a major financial success. It also forms the crucial evidence for the surviving reputation of the first film. The greatest compliment that *Terminator 2* pays to its predecessor is that it does much more than simply carry on the story. In a subtle and sophisticated way, it recapitulates and comments on it. Cameron was aware that *Terminator 2*, with a budget almost twenty times greater than its predecessor, had to be comprehensible to an audience who had never seen *The Terminator*. He also knew that a large part of his audience had seen *The Terminator* repeatedly on video and that they would pick up on the tiniest references.

The very first caption of *Terminator 2* – 'Los Angeles 2029' – is itself a shock, simply because it is the same caption that began *The Terminator*. Is this succession or recapitulation? This pre-credit sequence repeats a series of motifs and devices from the original: the cyborgs and flying ships, the ramshackle vehicles, the killings. Cameron is demonstrating his faithfulness to the original, but also showing how much more he can do this time around. Fans of the film knew about the limitations there had previously been in what Cameron could show us. The initial display of conspicuous consumption, with more ships, far more soldiers, and a whole army of cyborgs, promises us more than we got before. Cameron then surprises us again. In the original, John Connor was like Jesus in films like *Ben-Hur* – too important for us to see directly. Now we see him conducting a battle – paradoxically a battle which, as a result of what happens during the rest of the film, will never take place.

The first appearance of the terminator is once again a conscious reconstruction, down to the disturbance of the stray newspaper sheets on the ground in anticipation of the arrival. The scene is recreated in a pleasurable way but with more detail, more special effects and, as the scene progresses, the tongue firmly in the cheek. Even the first appearance of the terminator's computer display is a joke. The bar-room tough blows smoke in his face and the caption appears: 'scan carcinogen vapour'.

After the terminator of the Reagan years, this is evidently the kinder, gentler Schwarzenegger of the Bush administration. In the first film, he obtained his clothes by killing a punk in a vigilante act. Now he strolls into a Country and Western bar, itself a venue of cartoonish toughness. The cowboy parody is overt, and when the camera pans up his leather-clad body, when he purloins the bar owner's sunglasses and screeches away to the sound of blues music, we're meant to laugh and cheer.

Many of the slighter references to the previous film are slyly comic. The grisly psychiatrist, Silberman, fills in a group of his students about the institutionalisation of Sarah Connor: 'She believes that a machine called a terminator, which looks human of course, was sent back through time to kill her.' A student responds: 'That's original.' This is, one assumes, an unusually easygoing James Cameron joke about a scenario which was accused of many things, but never of excessive originality.

Grimly, we realise that Sarah has become Reese. She is now the one who is treated as mad, burdened by the pain of knowledge. Like Reese she is trained to kill but also tormented by dreams of the future.

Terminator 2

And later when she heads down to the hispanic world of California's southern border, we notice that she now speaks fluent Spanish, compared with her inability in the final scene of *The Terminator* even to ask for petrol without a phrasebook.

Terminator 2 contains visual references to its predecessor, often of the most frivolous and enjoyable kind, in almost every scene. The camera focuses on the motto of the LAPD, 'to serve and protect', with equal irony, whether it is at the moment when Reese steals a shotgun or when the T1000 steps out at the house of John Connor's fosterparents. We recognise the truck driven in pursuit of John Connor as a full-size version of the one that was crushed by the terminator's car before the murder of the first Sarah Connor. As before, the first encounter between the two time travellers, ends with Schwarzenegger being thrown through a window.

The lengthy explanations delivered by the terminator to John are a conscious recapitulation of Michael Biehn's notoriously indigestible explanations in *The Terminator* but Schwarzenegger is trumping Biehn by showing that he can do them better. He has the considerable advantage of delivering them without expression, much as Leonard Nimoy's Mr Spock was able to do. He is also given some better lines. In response to the question of who sent him, Schwarzenegger is able to say: 'You did. Thirty-five years from now.' Many of the jokes depend on shared memories. The terminator tells John that he can't go home because that is the place where the T1000 would try to reacquire him. Really? '*I* would,' he replied. A funny response, but funnier for those who remember that this is precisely what he did in the previous film. Slasher horror is now made comic.

Other echoes of *The Terminator* relate to the humanisation of the terminator in *Terminator 2*. After the famously laconic role in the first film, John instructs the terminator in teenage slang – no problemo; chill out; dickwad; hasta la vista, baby – thus parodying Schwarzenegger's penchant for catchphrases as well as providing him with them.

In a more sustained way, memories of the first film form an implied counterpoint to events in the second film. Cameron obviously expects a large section of his audience to be so familiar with *The Terminator* that they can register the constant ironies or contrasts. When, in what may be the best moment of *Terminator 2*, the terminator-imitating-John speaks to the T1000-imitating-John's foster-mother, we recognise it as a variation on the phone-call between Sarah Connor and the terminator-imitating-her mother. Only here John is saved from giving his whereabouts away.

Sometimes the references show Cameron consciously raising the stakes. What could be safer than the police station in *The Terminator*? The answer is a high-security mental hospital. The psychiatrist seems once more to be leaving just as the murderous terminator arrives. Will he get away with it again? At the last moment, gratifyingly, he is taken hostage by Sarah and forced to face up to the reality of the terminators. Where a cowering Sarah was previously dragged to safety by Michael Biehn, here she manages most of the escape by herself. When Michael Biehn came to see the sequel, he must have smiled ruefully at the moment in the asylum scene, when Schwarzenegger is given Biehn's own best line from the first film: 'Come with me, if you want to live.' Except that Schwarzenegger is given much more time in which to say it, one of the benefits of star power.

Cameron is aware of his responsibilities as the director of a hundred-million-dollar project that needs to appeal to everybody. So we get a chance to see Arnie toting an even larger gun than he had in *The Terminator* but we can, if we wish, also reassure ourselves that it is parodic. With almost chilling skill, Cameron sets out to redeem everything that might have seemed dark or irresponsible in his original film. When Sarah attempts to assassinate Dyson – and thus prevent him inventing the technology that will cause the nuclear holocaust – she becomes the terminator (just as the terminator is becoming human), even down to the orange dot of her laser sight on the back of his head. We didn't care much about the murders of the wrong Sarah Connor but we are now made to feel what it might be to kill someone you don't know.

Later in the same scene, the terminator is even allowed a redemptive version of the stripping of the flesh from his arm that we flinched at before. Now he is doing it, in praiseworthy fashion, as the only means of convincing Dyson of the truth of their story. During the shoot-out at the Cyberdyne headquarters, the terminator is even given a chance to deliver the 'I'll be back' line in a new, reassuring context, as Sarah and John are trapped in the exploded building. And sure enough he crashes back into the building with a police van, not to kill but to save. Presumably only considerations of time prevented him removing one of his eyes and donating it to a local home for blind orphans.

The final chase is a sustained reference to the chase at the same climactic point of *The Terminator*. The T1000's final line, like the terminator's, is 'Get out' but is delivered now not in the cab of a lorry but in the cockpit of a helicopter in flight. The chase is a parody in a variety of ways, and this time the lorry is carrying liquid nitrogen, appearing to freeze the terminator rather than to burn him up.

In the final battle in the factory, Sarah is given Arnie's phrase, 'Fuck you', where it is used, redemptively once more, as an assertion of maternal fidelity rather than of inhumanity. The terminator seems to have been destroyed, as Reese was at the end of *The Terminator*, and on a first viewing we expect that Sarah will triumph and blow the T1000 into the vat of molten metal. But just as we have already seen that, in this alienated modern world, a computer is a better father than the candidate furnished by the authorities, so he is also a better hero and he returns at the moment when Sarah runs out of ammunition. The curious moral seems to be that just as humans had so abnegated their responsibilities that they handed over the responsibility for their defence to a computer defence system, so they need a computer to save them as well. In the final recapitulation of the first film, Sarah presses the destruct button, but this time not as an act of assertion but as an acquiescence in the heroic self-immolation of Arnold Schwarzenegger.

Terminator 2 is a skilful entertainment, and confirmed that James Cameron is a master of the sequel. Perhaps he was educated by the experience of having his *Rambo: First Blood, Part II* script rewritten by Sylvester Stallone. Cameron's *Aliens* and *Terminator 2* are both excellent examples of how to be both faithful and unfaithful and original, notably superior to such sequels as *Predator 2* and *Die Harder*. But the sequel is a smaller thing than *The Terminator*. In the final scene, the terminator staggers forward after his doughty victory against the T1000: 'I need a vacation,' he says, in the final relinquishing of any pretence that this is not Arnie, winking at us with his one functioning eye. Amusing as he is, the terminator in *Terminator 2* has become a sitcom character, more Herman Munster than Boris Karloff, with his dry delivery of a line, his bemused attempts to master the oddities of suburban American life, his sententious 'but seriously' morals: 'It is in your nature to destroy yourselves.'

Among the shocks experienced on returning from *Terminator 2* to *The Terminator* is that it is about flesh as well as metal. The terminator isn't just burned away at the end of the film. He gradually decays and disintegrates from scene to scene, removing pieces of his body, decomposing. *Terminator 2* humanised the idea of the cyborg, made him civic minded, just as its star Schwarzenegger had made himself admired as a public figure above and beyond any of his individual films. But when President Schwarzenegger has entered the White House, *The Terminator* will still be there, unforgettable, untameable: the endoskeleton in his cupboard.

As for James Cameron himself, his career after *The Terminator* cannot help but seem a falling-off, but from his perspective what does this matter? When he began filming, he was a failing B-movie director on the edge of oblivion. While his critics sit at home writing about other people's films, James Cameron is in Hollywood with a fat production deal and final cut. Here, as in so many other ways, *The Terminator* achieved what it was meant to achieve.

Credits

THE TERMINATOR

USA

1984

Director
James Cameron

Production companies
Cinema '84, A Greenberg
Brothers Partnership, A
Pacific Western Production,
A Euro Film Funding Ltd.
Feature, An Orion Pictures
Release

Executive producers
John Daly, Derek Gibson

Producer
Gale Anne Hurd

Production executive
Bruce M. Kerner

Production co-ordinator
Kathy Breen

Production manager
Donna Smith

Location manager
Joseph A. Liuzzi

**Post-production
supervisor**
Donna Smith

Second unit directors
Jean-Paul Ouellette,
(effects) Stan Winson

Assistant directors
Betsy Magruder, Thomas
Irvine, Robert Roda

Screenplay
James Cameron, Gale
Anne Hurd

Additional dialogue
William Wisher Jnr.

Photography
Adam Greenberg

Colour process
CFI; prints by DeLuxe

Colour consultant
Peter Silverman

**Second unit
photographer**
Chuck Colwell

**Special visual effects
photographer**
John Huneck

Process photographer
Austin McKinney

Insert photographer
Anne Coffey

**Camera operator
(second unit)**
Sean McLin, Alec
Hirschfeld

Special visual effects
Fantasy II Film Effects,
(production supervisor)
Leslie Huntley

**Rear screen
projectionist**
Gerald McClain

Opticals
Ray Mercer and Company,
(effects) Image 3, Laurel
Klick, Phil Huff,
(consultant) Mark Sawicki

Matte artist
Ken Marschall

**Graphic animation
effects**
Ernest D. Farino

Editor
Mark Goldblatt

Associate editor
Michael Bloecher

Art director
George Costello

Set decorator
Maria Rebman Caso

Set dressers
Cindy Rebman, Greg Wolf

Scenic artists
Amy McGary, Kristen
McGary

Special effects supervisor
Gene Warren Jnr

Special effects co-ordinator
Ernest D. Farino

Special effects
Roger George, Frank DeMarco

Pyrotechnics and fire effects
Joseph Viskocil

Terminator special effects
Stan Winston (creator), Shane Mahan, Tom Woodruff, John Rosengrant, Richard Landon, Brian Wade, David Miller, Jack Bricker

Terminator mechanical effects
Ellis Burman Jnr., Bob Williams

Terminator stop motion
Peter Kleinow, (model) Doug Beswick

Models
Michael Joyce (supervising), Gary Rhodaback, Paul Kassler

GMF robot operated by
Ellison Machinery

Motoman robots operated by
Yaskawa Electric America

Music
Brad Fiedel

Music consultant
Budd Carr

Music post-production co-ordinator
Robert Randles

Music editor
Emilie Robertson

Songs
'You Can't Do That' by Ricky Phillips
'Photoplay' by Tahnee Cain, Pug Baker, Jonathan Cain
'Burnin' in the Third Degree' by Tahnee Cain, Mugs Cain, Dave Amato, Brett Tuggle, Ricky Phillips, performed by Tryanglz
'Pictures of You' by Jay Ferguson, performed by 16mm
'Intimacy' by Linn Van Hek, Joe Dolce, performed by Linn Van Hek

Costume design
Hilary Wright, (supervisor) Deborah Everton

Costumer (second unit)
Julia Gombert

Make-up
Jefferson Dawn, (second unit) Kyle Tucy

Title design
Ernest D. Farino

Supervising sound editor
David Campling

Sound recordist
Richard Lightstone

Sound re-recordists
Terry Porter, David J. Hudson, Mel Metcalfe

Sound effects editors
Gil Marchant, Jim Klinger, Jim Fritch, Greg Dillon, Horace Manzanares, Gary Shepherd, Mike Le Mare, Karola Storr, Rob Miller

Sound effects
Mayflower Films, (synthesised) Robert Garrett

Foley artists
Gordon Daniel, John Post

Production assistants
Scott Javine, (set) Deborah A. Hebert, George Parra, (special visual effects) Don Bland, Jane A. Pahlman, (second unit) Terry Benedict, (costumes) Virginia Hartman

Stunt co-ordinator
Ken Fritz

Stunts
Gary McLarty, Frank
Orsatti, Peter Turner, Tom
Hart, Gene Hartline, Hill
Farnsworth, Tony Cecere,
Jeff Dashnow, Marion
Green, Jim Stern, Jean
Malahni, J. Suzanne Fish

Animals
Birds and Animals
Unlimited

107 minutes
9,633 feet

Arnold Schwarzenegger
Terminator

Michael Biehn
Kyle Reese

Linda Hamilton
Sarah Connor

Paul Winfield
Traxler

Lance Henriksen
Vukovich

Rick Rossovich
Matt

Bess Motta
Ginger

Earl Boen
Silberman

Dick Miller
Pawn shop clerk

Shawn Schepps
Nancy

Bruce M. Kerner
Desk sergeant

Franco Columbu
Future terminator

Bill Paxton
Punk leader

**Brad Rearden, Brian
Thompson**
Punks

**William Wisher Jnr., Ken
Fritz, Tom Oberhaus**
Policemen

Ed Dogans
Cop in alley

Joe Farago
TV anchorman

Hettie Lynne Hurtes
TV anchorwoman

Tony Mirelez
Station attendant

**Philip Gordon, Anthony
J. Trujillo**
Mexican boys

Stan Yale
Derelict

**Al Kahn, Leslie Morris,
Hugh Farrington, Harriet**

**Medin, Loree Frazier,
James Ralston**
Customers

Norman Friedman
Cleaning man

Barbara Powers
Ticket taker

Wayne Stone
Tanker driver

David Pierce
Tanker partner

John E. Bristol
Phone booth man

Webster Williams
Reporter

Patrick Pinney
Bar customer

Bill W. Richmond
Bartender

Chino 'Fats' Williams
Truck driver

Gregory Robbins
Motel customer

Marianne Muellerleile
Wrong Sarah

John Durban
Sentry

BFI Modern Classics is an exciting new series which combines careful research with high quality writing about contemporary cinema. Authors write on a film of their choice, making the case for its elevation to the status of classic. The series will grow into an influential and authoritative commentary on all that is best in the cinema of our time.

If you would like to receive further information about future **BFI Modern Classics** or about other books on film, media and popular culture from BFI Publishing, please fill in your name and address and return this card to the BFI*.

No stamp needed if posted in the UK, Channel Islands, or Isle of Man.

NAME

ADDRESS

POSTCODE

* North America: Please return your card to:
Indiana University Press, Attn: LPB, 601 N Morton Street,
Bloomington, IN 47401-3797

BFI Publishing
21 Stephen Street
FREEPOST 7
LONDON
W1E 4AN